Original title:
Where the Walls Talk

Copyright © 2025 Creative Arts Management OÜ
All rights reserved.

Author: Isaac Ravenscroft
ISBN HARDBACK: 978-1-80587-047-0
ISBN PAPERBACK: 978-1-80587-517-8

Murmurs of Timeworn Rooms

Old chairs squeak with stories,
Whispers of long lost glories.
Pots and pans in a quiet clatter,
Spilling secrets that simply flatter.

Dust motes dance in sunlit beams,
Couches that remember dreams.
Walls chuckle as they hear the tales,
Of family feuds and puppy trails.

The Language of Cracks and Crevices

Cracks in plaster start to giggle,
Filling the air with a sly wiggle.
Crevices form their own delights,
Chirping jokes on lonely nights.

A cupboard sighs with weary winks,
As shelves share their saucy links.
Echoes prance with sassy cheer,
Making memories perfectly clear.

Fragments of Lives Lived

A faded frame holds laughter's light,
Watching antics from day to night.
Footprints tell of dances bold,
While laughter from the past unfolds.

Sticky notes on the fridge remind,
Of funny moments left behind.
Every scratch and tarnished spot,
Holds a giggle, just a lot!

Resonance of Lost Dreams

A trumpet mute still plays its tune,
Chasing echoes beneath the moon.
Old posters whisper dreams once grand,
While echoes laugh in happy band.

Mirrors crack with humorous grins,
Reflecting all our silly sins.
Each corner holds a gleeful tone,
As past loud laughter calls us home.

The Breaths Between the Bricks

In the corners, whispers dwell,
Secrets shared, they weave a spell.
Laughter echoes, a playful cheer,
Every creak, a tale to hear.

Footsteps shuffle, a rhythmic dance,
Walls wobble, they take a chance.
Jokes exchanged in silent glee,
A comedy of bricks, oh so free!

Peeking out from patches worn,
Stories bloom from each forlorn.
Chimneys chuckle, chiming in,
A wall's grin holding hidden sin.

Nooks and crannies, rich with jest,
Every crack, a hidden quest.
With a wink, they keep their score,
In this home, who needs a door?

Tracing the Legacy in Dust

Amidst the cobwebs, dust takes flight,
Chasing shadows, day and night.
Fleeting memories swirl and twirl,
Like a pirouette, they dance and curl.

Footprints linger, stories neat,
Dusty saga beneath our feet.
In the air, laughter sticks,
As history laughs at its own tricks.

With every sweep, tales get bold,
Moldy jokes from times of old.
A maze of echoes, rich and bright,
As the dust winks in delight.

Ghostly giggles chase the broom,
Revealing legends in the gloom.
In every speck, a chuckle's held,
As dust devils dance, enchanted and quelled.

Chronicles of the Captivated Walls

In every seam, a secret nudges,
Buried tales, the wall begrudges.
Tales of cats and midnight snacks,
An old shoe and a pair of slacks.

Colors peel, but laughter stays,
Echoing through our silly ways.
In the silence, they exchange,
Comedic plays, a little strange.

Tales of mishaps, love in doubt,
Walls giggle when we pout.
With every thump, their voices blend,
A merry band that'll never end.

If only bricks could laugh and sing,
What wild tales could they bring?
In their company, we can't ignore,
A house of joy, forevermore!

Dialogues of Dust and Dreams

In corners where shadows play,
Dust bunnies dance, what a display.
They gossip of shoes, lost and found,
And tumble on flooring, round and round.

A chair creaks with stories to tell,
Of a cat who thought it could spell.
It wrote on the rug with style and grace,
But letters turned into a chase.

The clock on the wall takes a snooze,
While cobwebs weave their own ruse.
Every tick and tock, a giggle escapes,
As time trips over its own silly shapes.

The mirror grins, with secrets to share,
It caught a mime making faces in air.
Laughter echoes through space and time,
In an old house, every joke's a rhyme.

Echoes of Forgotten Stories

In the attic, a trunk bursts wide,
With costumes of laughter tucked inside.
A pirate hat, a tutu bright,
They throw a party every night.

The wall clock chuckles with each tick,
While an old typewriter plays a trick.
It types out jokes with clacking keys,
And makes the old wallpaper sneeze.

The window frames chat with the breeze,
Sharing tales of the neighborhood trees.
They laugh at squirrels and birds that squawk,
In a language only they can talk.

Underneath, the floorboards creak and groan,
But add their own humor to the tone.
It's a symphony of jests and quirks,
Where every plank knows how it works.

Whispers Beneath the Paint

Beneath layers of vintage hues,
Lies a dance of secrets and silly clues.
The paint cracks in laughter's embrace,
Revealing the quirkiest stories with grace.

A room full of laughter, echoes abound,
Each brush stroke whispers, "Look what I found!"
A cat with a crown in a pink polka dot,
And a dog that plays chess? Oh, what a shot!

A tiny mouse, brave and spry,
Sneaks out each night to dance and fly.
He waltzes with shadows on the walls,
While dust settles down and gently falls.

The laughter inside these four chilly walls,
Wraps around like soft, cozy shawls.
In whispers and giggles, it starts to paint,
A mural of memories, chipper and quaint.

Secrets in Solid Frames

The pictures hung, in solemn rows,
Hold secrets that no one quite knows.
A smile peeks out from the frame,
As the background blends in with the game.

The sofa speaks of past land shifts,
Of crumbs lost in gabby rifts.
Friends once plopped, tales were spun,
About clumsy moves, and races fun.

A lamp chuckles with an electric gleam,
It lights up the past like a dream.
Casting shadows that dance with delight,
Making even the mute paintings ignite.

Each corner holds a giggling ghost,
At family gatherings, they toast.
To the stories framed in color and light,
Where laughter keeps everything bright!

Echoes of Silent Sentinels

In the corner, a paint chip grins,
It tells tales of the places it's been.
With laughter, it dances, a playful sprite,
Sharing secrets through the edge of night.

The floorboards creak like an old man's laugh,
Telling stories in a crooked half.
Each squeak a punchline, each thud a cheer,
As echoes of yesteryear bounce near.

Whispers in the Crumbling Corners

In the crannies, a dust cloud twirls,
Conspiring with shadows and giggling girls.
They swipe at the sunlight, laugh out loud,
While their joy gathers dust, so very proud.

A cobweb's tangled laughter rings,
Flitting through darkness on delicate wings.
It catches the moonlight, a net of fun,
Spinning tales till the morning's begun.

Secrets Embedded in Brick

A brick with a crack holds a haughty grin,
Like it knows all the whoppers, where to begin.
Each chip in its face tells of mischief and play,
Of feet that have stumbled then danced away.

And the mortar between seems to chuckle in sync,
As it watches us wonder and skeptically think.
With every small shift and every sly glance,
The walls seem to urge us to join in the dance.

Conversations of the Aged Edifice

The roof starts to chatter in a cheeky tone,
Comparing its shingles to smooth granite stone.
'I'm older, I'm wiser,' the chimney will brag,
While a squirrel in the eaves starts to giggle and wag.

The windows wink softly, sharing a jest,
Of curious neighbors who stop for a rest.
A breeze through the cracks whispers jokes and more,
As the house joins the fun, raucous at its core.

Interludes of Forgotten Echoes

In the hallway, whispers prance,
A shoe's misstep—a clumsy dance.
Pictures grin with a cheeky grin,
As if they know where we have been.

The curtains flutter, gossip flies,
A tale of socks that twist and tie.
Lampshades giggle in soft light,
Their stories spark the silly night.

Old chairs creak with a funny sigh,
As if they know just how to lie.
The clock ticks off with teasing grace,
Reminding us to quicken pace.

So in this home of jests and glee,
Even the floorboards chuckle with me.
A world alive with playful smirk,
In every nook, there's magic at work.

The Tapestry of Tempting Tales

Woven threads of laughter bright,
Each corner holds a funny sight.
The doorbell chimes with playful cheer,
It rings like friends who linger near.

A rug disguised as a cheeky beast,
Underfoot, a bumpy feast.
The plants conspire to steal the show,
Their leaves nodding as if to know.

Walls adorned with silly hats,
Mice in pockets and laughing cats.
Every nook hums a mirthful tune,
Lights flicker like a dancing moon.

So step inside this humored space,
Where laughter weaves a warm embrace.
In every stitch, a story blooms,
A tapestry where joy consumes.

Lyrical Walls that Listen

Upon the walls, a laughter stream,
Echoes of each silly dream.
Nooks and crannies crack a smile,
Sharing secrets all the while.

The windows wink, the doors confer,
As if they've heard each little stir.
The floorboards squeak with knowing glee,
Sharing tales of 'Who sat, who frees?'

Mortar and stone join in the fun,
As if they've nibbled on a bun.
They hum along to the lightest jest,
As every crevice plays its best.

So let your laughter fill this space,
For every wall is a friendly face.
A concert hall for giggles sweet,
Where humor and joy together meet.

The Ballad of Buried Secrets

A dusty diary whispers low,
Of all the antics years ago.
Each shelf holds laughter in a jar,
And tells of mishaps near and far.

Beneath the stairs, old shoes converse,
Their stories getting far more terse.
A hat forgotten, plump with tales,
Of windy days, and wild gales.

The old piano hums a tune,
Of mischief played beneath the moon.
Notes flutter like giddy birds,
As laughter lingers, swift like words.

So dive into this playful trove,
Where antics flourish, secrets rove.
In every crack, a tale is spun,
A funny ballad; let's have fun.

The Remnants of Rhyme

In corners where the echoes play,
A sock once lost now holds a sway.
Whispers weave through cracks and seams,
Tickling dust as if in dreams.

Leftovers of laughter linger still,
As old boards creak with every thrill.
A cat in a corner snores with glee,
While boxes plot a grand ol' spree.

Jokes unspooled from history's thread,
The fridge hums jokes that once were said.
Paint peels with a giggle and sigh,
As memories dance and no one knows why.

Inscriptions of Inhabited Spaces

On the wall where the scribbles grow,
A love note wedged where no one goes.
Kids drew monsters with crayons bright,
Now they giggle in ghostly light.

A calendar hangs with days gone by,
Marking pizza nights and winks from the sky.
The stains of laughter, spilled drinks galore,
Trace commentary on life's long score.

Beneath the table, an old shoe lies,
With stories sewn in its laces' ties.
Hidden humor floods every nook,
If you listen close, just take a look.

Stories Etched in Shadows

Shadows dance when the sun runs late,
Chasing tales that we can narrate.
A lamp that flickers has quite the tale,
Of wild parties and a cat that wails.

Spiders spin webs filled with yarn,
Entangling the air with a sitcom charm.
A broom winks slyly, it knows the score,
Of dust bunnies hiding forevermore.

Reflections laugh in the mirror's gaze,
Each crack a story of silly days.
If only walls had ears and smiles,
They'd share a tale after a million miles.

The Echo of Unseen Lives

Voices ripple through the room,
As ghosts of breakfasts start to bloom.
A chair that squeaks with too much pride,
Holds all the tales it can't confide.

In the hallway, echoes play tag,
Hiding from laughter and the old rag.
Footsteps trace the patterns spun,
Of family antics and grandma's fun.

Picture frames smile with eyes so wide,
Stealing the moments we can't abide.
A dance through time in worn-out shoes,
Where unseen lives are the best we choose.

Stories of Stone and Wood

In a house that grins and leans,
Laughter bounces off the beams.
A chair hiccups, a table sighs,
As secrets dance beneath the skies.

The bricks tell tales of ghostly socks,
While curtains giggle at passing mocks.
A door creaks loud, it's in on the fun,
Whispers of pancakes, not yet done.

The floors, they rumble with playful feet,
While shadows skip to a lively beat.
Tales of tricks and silly pranks,
Echoing joy in the empty ranks.

In every nook, a moment shines,
With punchlines tossed like wishing lines.
From window sills, laughs take flight,
A home alive, in giggles bright.

Chronicles Beneath the Ceiling

Up above, the light fixtures buzz,
Not with work, but with a buzz.
Each flicker tells a chuckling tale,
Of late-night snacks and soda stale.

With every thump of the overhead fan,
A funny story begins to span.
The textures hold the jests so well,
Whispering jokes no tongue can tell.

From the beams come sighs of delight,
As memories dance in the soft light.
The laughter lingers, a playful tease,
In this chamber of silliness, nothing's a breeze.

Under the ceiling, where stories twirl,
Life's silly moments in a happy whirl.
Each corner hides a grin or two,
In this space, humor brews anew.

Shadows that Sing of Youth

Shadows prance across the floor,
Chasing each other, longing for more.
In corners where the light does fade,
Silly dances, memories made.

A youthful grin from the old clock chimes,
Ticking and tocking with playful rhymes.
Each second a giggle, a wink, a tease,
As playful ghosts move with such ease.

The mirror laughs at the mess we've made,
With hairbrushes tossed and dreams displayed.
Reflecting youth in all its charm,
While shadows weave a yarn, disarm.

In the flickering lights, a party begins,
Where laughter's echo never thins.
Each shadow sings a cheerful tune,
Under the watch of a playful moon.

Echo Chamber of Memories

In the hall, echoes bounce and play,
Memories join in a grand ballet.
The laughter rings, a joyful shout,
As silly tales float in and out.

An echo of socks that danced in pairs,
Underneath life's light-hearted layers.
The shutters clap with every joke,
While shadows giggle and softly poke.

Retold adventures from years gone by,
Each chuckle a twinkle in the eye.
The corners blush from the tales they hear,
As time stands still, with all its cheer.

In this chamber filled with delight,
Every moment shines, oh so bright.
With echoes of laughter, stories unfold,
In this space, life's joys are retold.

Legacies Encoded in Layers

In a house with quite the flair,
Squeaky floors that make you stare,
Ghosts argue who was first in line,
One claims the attic, the other, divine.

They toss around old dusty hats,
Argue over where to store the bats,
A poltergeist spills tea with glee,
While someone yells, 'That's not for me!'

Behind each crack, a tale unfolds,
Of parties mishap and ancient moulds,
Nonsense echoes through the halls,
Whispers of fortunes, mishaps, and falls.

Laughter lingers where silence was,
Jokes trade places with phantom buzz,
In quirky homes where spirits dwell,
They share their jokes, oh, quite the swell!

The Ghostwriter's Canvas

In a study where shadows leap,
A ghost with a quill without much sleep,
He scribbles tales of snacks and tricks,
Of parties, laughter, and old politics.

His parchment's filled with ancient glee,
Of silly jokes and a cat named Dee,
With every stroke, he shakes with mirth,
"Did you hear about the ghost on Earth?"

He writes of walls that hum and sing,
Of a past where furniture wore bling,
His pen dances like a lively breeze,
A specter's wit with zest to tease.

In this abode, stories intertwine,
With glimpses of chaos, all so fine,
The ghost laughs as he crafts his art,
With a wink at the living, oh, such a start!

Resonant Chronicles

In a corner where shadows blend,
A cheeky ghost plays with a friend,
They juggle memories, loud and bright,
As walls chuckle at a silly sight.

"Remember the time you danced with flair?"
The ghost proclaims, "You fell in a chair!"
Laughter echoes through the painted air,
As furniture groans, "You had no care!"

Each crack in the wall, a giggle ensues,
As the bathroom mirror shares old clues,
A duet of laughter, time intertwined,
Spinning tales of those left behind.

As the clock ticks, tales take flight,
The walls of laughter ignite the night,
With every joke, they shimmer and sway,
In this house, they play every day!

Echoes of Yesterday

In a room filled with peppy cheer,
Walls whisper tales we long to hear,
A chair with sass claims its own space,
While broken pots compete in the race.

They gossip loud about pie recipes,
And argue over who stole the freeze,
A playful skirmish of silly prides,
As history spills from relics that hide.

A ghostly voice joins in the fun,
"Remember the time we ran with the sun?"
With echoes of laughter that bounce and gleam,
They're crafting a most joyful dream.

So join the ruckus, let spirits sway,
In this timeless frolic, come and play,
For every wall holds a whimsical spark,
In a world where laughter ignites the dark!

Where Timefolds in the Quiet

In the corners, secrets thrive,
A cat's meow, a ghost's high five.
Old chairs laugh as they creak,
Each echo tells stories unique.

Paint peels like a faded joke,
Tickling thoughts as the silence spoke.
A clock's hand dances, hilariously slow,
Time's a clown in this quiet show.

Dust bunnies hold a wild debate,
Who'll tell the tale of a missing plate?
The ceiling whispers old friends' names,
While sunlight plays silly light games.

A spider spins a web so tight,
Trapping giggles in beams of light.
In every crack, a jest unfolds,
As laughter weaves through stories told.

Song of the Faded Wallpaper

The paper peels like an old band,
Notes forgotten, dust on the stand.
Every pattern has a giggle hidden,
From flowers that danced, now forbidden.

Each swirl speaks of laughter past,
Full of quirks, made to last.
A patch of teal, and then a red,
Colors of laughter overhead.

In the fray, ghosts waltz and spin,
Joining in on the joyful din.
Every wrinkle tells of glee,
Can you hear the jubilee?

Beneath the surface, tales unfold,
Adventures bright, never old.
So let's rejoice, let's repair the thread,
In the dance of the colors, mischief spread!

Lives Lived in Hushed Whispers

In twilight rooms, they softly plot,
Mice in slippers, giving it a shot.
Walls listen close to every scheme,
Sharing chuckles in a cozy dream.

The floorboards creak with a sly remark,
As shadows play in the fading dark.
A pair of shoes with untold tales,
Squeak secrets shared like old gales.

Curtains rustle, eavesdropping tight,
On the banter of the starry night.
Whispers flutter, giggles bounce,
As time twirls in an airy flounce.

In hidden nooks, the stories gleam,
A silly history, a bright-eyed theme.
So let's gather 'round for a chat,
With giggles and tales where we all sat.

The Breath of the Building

Old bricks chuckle, in soft repose,
As echoes tickle from toes to nose.
Windows wink at the passerby,
Sharing whispers as they sigh.

The staircase sings with every stomp,
A melody ruffled—a rhythmic romp.
Light spills laughter through cracked panes,
While shadows dance in silly chains.

Chimneys puff and puff with glee,
An old dog snorts—what could that be?
Each crack and crevice, a giggle found,
In this ancient house, joy abounds.

Every inch has a playful grin,
As the walls chuckle thick and thin.
So let's toast to this lively air,
Where the silliness flows everywhere!

Ghosts of Past Lives

In corners, whispers seep,
Old socks yell, 'Don't sleep!'
The chairs all try to chat,
About the ghostly cat.

The curtains sway and grin,
As ancient tales begin,
They speak of love and strife,
In a comical life.

Beneath the creaky floor,
Lies legends, never bore,
Of socks that dance at night,
In a lively, silly fright.

The past gives quite a show,
With silent laughs that flow,
So when you hear a squeak,
Just know the walls can speak!

The Poetry of Weathered Stone

Oh stones with stories vast,
They hold a hearty laugh,
Each crack a tale to share,
Of muddy kids, where's the care?

They've seen the silliest sights,
Like birds in sock fights,
With moss that looks like hats,
And ants that dance like sprats.

A whisper from the past,
'Why's the sky so vast?'
The stones just shrug and grin,
As shadows let the fun begin.

In every groove and line,
A punchline here to find,
Those rugged rocks, so bold,
Tell jokes of ages old!

Memories Encased in Plaster

The plaster knows your fears,
It stifles all your cheers,
'Tis thick with tales profound,
Like moans from underground.

It holds the scent of pies,
And laughter-filled goodbyes,
The accidents of youth,
Like gum stuck to a tooth.

One memory, quite absurd,
Of gossiping with a bird,
While watching paint peel down,
And dreaming of the town.

In layers, secrets hide,
A banter wild and wide,
So next time there's a crack,
The humor's coming back!

Sagas of Stained Glass

The glass, a storybook bright,
Tells tales of day and night,
With colors that all clash,
And ghosts who love to splash.

Sunlight gives a wink,
While shadows start to think,
'This window needs a dance,
To set the mood, enhance!'

It whispers in the breeze,
'Look at those silly trees,'
While raindrops, like confetti,
Join in, 'Aren't we ready?'

The narratives it weaves,
Bring chuckles, if you'd believe,
So when next you gaze and stare,
Remember, they're all there!

Palettes of the Past

In every corner, stories hide,
Painted whispers, where jesters bide.
Bright hues of laughter on faded walls,
Echoes of mischief in the playful calls.

A pink polka dot once graced a chair,
Fell into a dance without a care.
An orange cat, with a dapper coat,
Pretended to play the violin, but just wrote a quote.

A blue vase grinned as it held the breeze,
While a purple rug tangled with teasing sees.
A canvas of memories, brilliantly stark,
Gallery of giggles, they leave their mark.

Silhouettes Behind Closed Doors

Behind those doors, shadows exchange,
Conversations quirky, wonderfully strange.
A curious cat, peeking in fright,
Opens the scene, to a comical sight.

A chair with a hat takes a bow so thick,
Swaying side to side, like it's in a flick.
Lampshades giggle, whispering tales,
Of socks mismatched and fairy tale fails.

An old broom sings 'It's a dirty job!'
While candles flicker, ready to sob.
The silhouettes dance, waltzing in cheer,
In the house of laughter, where no one's near.

The Archive of Echoes

In a dusty archive where echoes collide,
Old furniture chuckles, and memories bide.
A spicy old chair cracks a witty joke,
While a tapestry blushes, its fibers provoke.

The clock on the wall, with a mischievous tick,
Counts all the giggles, rediscovers the trick.
Jars filled with laughter, stacked up so high,
Bellowing secrets to the curious fly.

A sofa flops down, pretending to snore,
Till the rug says, "Wake up! There's fun in store!"
Together they giggle, a raucous delight,
In this archive of echoes, where shadows unite.

Harmonies of the Heedless

In a wacky room, where chaos reigns,
Walls sing of folly, and silliness gains.
A violin cracked, but plays all day,
While mismatched socks join in the sway.

A broomstick pokes at the ceiling's soft fluff,
While drapes in the corner say, "That's enough!"
Echoing whims of harmony loud,
Creating a ruckus that gathers a crowd.

The pictures conspire, with grins oh so wide,
Whispering tales of the world's funny side.
In the land of the heedless, where laughter is found,
The symphony of silliness knows no bound.

Murmurs of the Inhabitants Past

In the corner, whispers play,
A sock puppet holds court all day.
The portraits grin with mischief anew,
Even the clock tickles time askew.

A hat on a shelf starts to prance,
Telling tales of an old sock dance.
The ghost of a sandwich lingers near,
It's perfectly fine, we just have beer!

The cat in the window's giving a speech,
To the dust bunnies, hoping to teach.
Old chairs creak with tales to impart,
As the radiator warms up its heart.

In every crack, there's laughter and glee,
As shadows play hide-and-seek with the bees.
Each nook and cranny knows how to jest,
In this funny haunt, we're truly blessed.

Labyrinths of Lost Conversations

On the stairs, echoes trip and fall,
Bananas in pajamas are having a ball.
The wallpaper flirts with the ceiling fan,
In a debate about whom they can ban.

Over in the hall, a lightbulb hums,
Reciting jokes in jumbled sums.
Mice scurry past, on a mission of fun,
While the fridge proposes a midnight run.

A chair mutters secrets, so bold and loud,
The rafters listen, part of the crowd.
There's a mirror, it chuckles at its own face,
In the comedy show of this odd place.

The rug plays coy, sliding its way,
While the pizza box tries to save the day.
With each whimsy, laughter unfolds,
And curtains of nonsense are joyfully rolled.

Unfolding Histories Within

Around the corner, a stool tells a tale,
Of the time it almost set off a gale.
The ceiling drips with laughter so sweet,
As an old boot jives with the beat.

A newspaper crinkles, sharing the news,
Of a cat who refuses to choose.
The paint peels with glee, plotting a caper,
While the spoons giggle under a paper.

In the attic, a trunk discusses its dreams,
Of dancing daylights and moonlit themes.
With a twinkle of dust, it starts to reminisce,
About the time it snoozed and lost its bliss.

The windows laugh, filling the air,
As the walls poke fun without a care.
In this world of whispers and cheerful notes,
Every crevice hums, spinning jokes.

The Narrative of the Nonexistent

An imaginary friend waves from the wall,
Sipping on lemonade, having a ball.
The furniture whispers secrets untold,
Of a party that still hasn't grown old.

The dust motes pirouette in the beam,
Like a troupe rehearsing in a vivid dream.
A shadow chortles, plotting a prank,
While the flowers tease, "Have you even drank?"

Behind a coat, an argument brews,
Over who wore it best, Carl or the blues?
The floorboards sway, bursting with pride,
As they host a shindig inside each stride.

The moonlight giggles, casting a smile,
As even the cobwebs make fun of style.
In this realm of fables and laughter galore,
Each story unfolds, begging for more.

Soliloquies of the Old Hearth

The old fireplace whispers tales,
Of burnt marshmallows and runaway snails.
Sparks dance in the embers' light,
As the cat plots a midnight flight.

The kettle's gossip fills the air,
It's about the toaster's wild love affair.
With crumbs as witness, they wink and tease,
Old furniture stifles just to freeze.

Old socks hide secrets snug in a fold,
Of adventures in the laundry, brave and bold.
Each stitch has laughter stitched in tight,
As socks slip away in the dead of night.

So gather 'round this hearth so grand,
Where laughter echoes and stories stand.
In every nook, a jest resides,
As we listen close where humor hides.

Nostalgia in the Narrow Halls

In narrow halls, echoes play,
Of squeaky shoes on a lively day.
Walls chuckle softly, they can't contain,
The sound of kids and their silly games.

They say the wallpaper knew the best,
Of pillow fights and treasure quests.
It's witnessed giggles and the chase,
As laughter dances in every space.

The dust bunnies wink—a furry crowd,
As each prank is cheered, oh so loud.
Every corner can't resist a sigh,
Of memories that tickle, flutter by.

So let's stroll through this winding lane,
Where every bend brings joy and pain.
These tales, they linger, funny and sweet,
In nostalgia's grasp, we're ever discreet.

The Archive of Abandoned Spaces

In corners where time has lost its way,
Ghosts of toys choose to forever stay.
A tricycle rusts, it laughs at fate,
While dolls hold court, a grand estate.

Old shoes stacked high, in a wobbly tower,
Plot journeys anew, hour by hour.
The cupboard hums tunes of the old days,
Where mismatched socks held grand ballets.

A spider spins plots, intricate and sly,
Stealing glances as we tiptoe by.
Creaky floors sing a playful tune,
While shadows giggle beneath the moon.

In these spaces, laughter is sewn,
With memories of a world much known.
Embrace the silliness, let it be,
As these abandoned hearts laugh joyfully.

Unwritten Poems in the Plaster

In the old walls, stories hide,
Whispers of laughter, proudly inside.
Pockmarks hold remnants of silly fights,
Eras past, like mischievous sprites.

The plaster dreams of things unsaid,
Of sock puppets and playful dread.
Vivid scenes paint playful sights,
Where shadows giggle deep into nights.

A ghost of a cat, spectrally prowls,
Stakes her claim to these echoing halls.
Yet no one scolds for mischief here,
Just cheeky smiles and hearty cheer.

So let's etch verses in laughter's own ink,
Awash in dreams, no need to think.
These unwritten poems, a joyous spree,
Forever linger, wild and free.

The Dialogue of Decay

In cracks the voices twist and twine,
Paint peels off, but it's just fine.
The echoes laugh at tales gone stale,
Where squirrels plot, and cats regale.

A door squeaks like it's in a play,
In whispered tones it has its say.
With every groan and subtle creak,
These walls are quirky, so to speak.

Lampshades drip with gossip old,
In shadows deep, their secrets told.
A chair that's wobbly drops some shade,
It can't hold in the tales it's made.

Dust bunnies dance, they've got a scheme,
The floors are soft; it's quite the dream.
They chuckle softly, just take a peek,
As the ceiling hums its hasty cheek.

Timeless Narratives

A window sighs with stories grand,
Of lovebirds lost and life unplanned.
Mismatched curtains take a stare,
At dreams that linger in the air.

The wallpaper laughs with every crease,
Each tear a joke, a sweet release.
The old clock winks, tickling time,
Its chimes a giggle, a light rhyme.

With every step, the floors confide,
Of messy spills and warmth inside.
A rusty nail makes a case with flair,
For each small drama, none too rare.

A shelf that creaks recalls spring blooms,
While dust motes dance in sunlit rooms.
Each nook reveals a crafted jest,
In every whisper, the walls are blessed.

Eavesdropping on Eternity

Cracks in the tiles hold secrets tight,
They gossip gently, day and night.
Old pictures smirk; frames roll their eyes,
As memories spike with sweet surprise.

The radiator chuckles with a hiss,
At lovers' fights and playful bliss.
Knobs that rattle add to the fun,
As beams hold meetings, one by one.

The attic hums with tales so old,
Of things unseen, and treasure untold.
A curtain sways, a knowing grin,
Inviting legends to tumble in.

With every shudder, walls confide,
An echo here, a flat out slide.
Beneath the paint, the tales persist,
As giggles spark in a dusty mist.

Tales in Tangled Vines

Vines crawl up, their stories climb,
Twisting and turning, a leafy rhyme.
Each tendril tells of sunlit days,
Of bees that hum in floral plays.

Wood creeps silently, clutching the past,
In this silent venue, shadows cast.
Branches swipe at the soft blue sky,
Whispering jokes that flutter by.

A trellis stands with a smirk so wise,
Holding laughter beneath the skies.
Between the leaves, a chatter's found,
As flowers pop to join the round.

Beneath the blooms, the earth abounds,
With silly tales and playful sounds.
Each twist of leaf and root evokes,
A symphony of happy folks.

Unraveling the Fabric of Time

In halls of whispers, secrets peek,
Old portraits giggle, then start to speak.
Time travels on, in a comical race,
Each tick a chuckle, each tock a face.

The grandfather clock tells jokes of old,
While the wallpaper dances, shy yet bold.
Rugs share tales of feet that tripped,
As laughter echoes, and records flip.

Loosening threads of yesteryear,
Mismatched minutes, all we hold dear.
A sock, a shoe, they tell their plight,
In stitches of joy, through day and night.

So listen closely; they all conspire,
With every crack, there's humor to inspire.
For every wall, a story, you'll find,
When the clock's tickling, you'll unwind your mind.

Murals of Memory Made Flesh

On these painted walls, a story unfurls,
Colors in laughter, like playful swirls.
Each brushstroke giggles, a wink from the past,
In murals alive, memories are cast.

Ceilings with ceilings, tales pile high,
The floorboards creak, as if asking why.
Mice wear sunglasses, snickering about,
While cats plot schemes, there's no need to pout.

Laughter's the pigment that colors the air,
Walls dressed in humor, a quirky affair.
With ghosts holding hands, in a dance they collide,
In the gallery's glow, absurdities glide.

A canvas of chaos, where echoes reside,
Tickling spines, where secrets abide.
Funny how memories, vibrant and bold,
Get caught in the paint, a sight to behold.

The Soul Beneath the Surface

Beneath the veneer, what do walls hide?
A snicker here, a gaffe with pride.
The patter of feet that just can't dance,
In corners they rumble, given a chance.

plaster crumbles, revealing the jest,
Fishnets of laughter, put worries to rest.
With echoes of giggles, they lift the gloom,
To shadows in corners, a playful room.

When the windows chat with curtains on spree,
Their banter lifts spirits, sets laughter free.
A tickle down the spine, as echoes persist,
With each creak and groan, humor is missed.

The soul of the space drinks in the light,
In echoes and chuckles, the mood feels right.
Let's dance with the ghosts of forgotten lore,
As they sip from the cup, they giggle and roar.

Verses of the Unseen

In shadows unseen, where whispers collide,
Chairs gossip softly, with nowhere to hide.
A patchwork of laughter, tucked in each seam,
Living in verses that bubble and beam.

Windows peek out, like curious spies,
Collecting the tales of the passersby.
Doors creak in laughter, like old friends do,
With visions of mischief in shades of blue.

From cracks in the paneling, tales take flight,
As splinters of joy dance in the light.
Each phrase a balloon, that floats up to grace,
The walls full of chuckles, in this happy place.

In a language of echoes, they banter all night,
The unseen writes verses of pure delight.
So listen, dear heart, to the unspoken fun,
For the walls have their stories, a tale yet begun.

Ink of Time on Tattered Floors

Footsteps dance on splintered wood,
A secret symphony, misunderstood.
Old paint peels with tales to share,
Laughs trapped in shadows, hanging in air.

Pigeons gossip on the window sill,
Whispering tales with corn and thrill.
The clock winks, tickles the floor,
Where shuffle and scuffle open the door.

A cat with dreams of far-off lands,
Stretches out as the world expands.
Dust bunnies giggle, the corners smile,
Each crack a story, each room a style.

Time scribbles notes on crooked beams,
Chasing after invisible dreams.
Let's laugh at life, embrace the quirk,
For every squeak, there's a hidden perk.

Heartbeats Imprinted on the Foundations

In the basement, echoes of a snack,
Where pizza parties sparked a laugh attack.
The floorboards creak like giggling friends,
Sharing secrets that nobody mends.

Planters whisper of misplaced seeds,
Allergies arise from the funniest deeds.
Screens flicker tales of the past,
Yet the best ones fade away fast.

A family dog wears memories grand,
Paws etched with love, a loyal band.
Heartbeats thump within the brick,
Timeless love, the perfect trick.

Through the windows, sunlight slips,
Revealing laughter through playful quips.
Foundations rumble with joyous sounds,
In every corner, affection abounds.

Murmuring in the Midst of Silence

In corners where cobwebs flutter play,
Whispers of mischief float every day.
Chairs slide back with a comedic jolt,
Invisible characters, a theatrical vault.

The fridge hums jokes through the night,
Boozy bottles chuckle, oh what a sight!
Eggs in a carton, plotting a prank,
With each devilish plan, they giggle and tank.

The light bulb flickers, plays peek-a-boo,
As shadows dance in a wacky crew.
Distant shuffles, a wild, loud cheer,
Murmuring echoes, a party here!

Under the stairs, the dust bunnies play,
Poking fun at the light of day.
In silence, laughter fills every space,
For the walls keep secrets, with a smile on their face.

Past Lives in Present Walls

Once a kitchen where chaos reigned,
Now a museum of nostalgia regained.
Each bruise on the wall has a tale to tell,
Of spills and chills, and laughter that fell.

The old sofa whispers of love's embrace,
As crumbs and glitter fill every place.
Ghosts of birthdays and ice cream fights,
In corners, we find the best highlights.

Tattered curtains sway with past regrets,
Yet their sighs turn to laughter, no frets.
The echoes of yesteryears' guests collide,
In a raucous reunion where memories reside.

So let's toast to the walls, the past they store,
Each scratch a giggle, every stain a roar.
For life within these confines shall last,
A funny tale woven with shadows cast.

Conversations of the Abandoned

In a house left behind, dust bunnies roam,
They plot silly pranks while I'm stuck at home.
A chair wiggles and then starts to sway,
Silly furniture, just wants to play!

The fridge hums jokes that I cannot hear,
It whispers the secrets of all who were near.
A pot knocks twice, then starts to dance,
What good's a ghost if it can't shake a chance?

Old socks hold debates on who wore them best,
They've got unmatched flair and a sense of jest.
Walls giggle softly, echoing cheer,
In this lively abode, I'm the only one here!

At night, the calendar holds a wild bash,
With parties of paper that make quite the splash.
Who knew that alone could be such a treat?
These abandoned chats really can't be beat!

Tales from Tattered Corners

In corners so dusty, stories unfold,
Of socks going missing and tea parties bold.
A cat plays the piano, then falls in a heap,
With laughter and whiskers, it puts me to sleep.

The wallpaper whispers, 'Remember that guy?'
Who danced with the radish that grew in the pie.
They chuckle at shadows that flop and that flail,
As the dust motes whirl like a chubby snail.

A cracked mirror winks, it's a jester in glass,
Reflecting my face—oh dear! What a sass!
With every crack, it tells tales of glee,
As it fractures my belly like chips on a spree.

The wallpaper peels with a giggle and snort,
Challenging cobwebs to a playful retort.
Where giggles abide and silliness reigns,
In these tattered corners, laughter remains!

Shadows of Unspoken Memories

In the dim light, shadows do sway,
Whispering secrets of things gone astray.
A broom joins in, sweeping tales of its own,
Of dust bunnies caught in a heart-shaped zone.

The calendar grins, with days all askew,
Marking the time when I spilled all my stew.
It chuckles aloud at my kitchen misdeeds,
As shadows converge, planting funny seeds.

Old window panes frame a giggling spree,
As curtains debate 'who can dance with glee?'
While pictures applaud from their frames on the wall,
With timeless banter, they echo the call.

In unspoken quirks, memories blush,
Filling the air with a soft, joyous hush.
In this room, it's clear that silence can sing,
As shadows throw parties, oh what joy they bring!

Voices in the Silence

In an empty room, the voices take flight,
A sock sings of journeys and tales of the night.
An echoing giggle darts in from the hall,
While the walls grin at the fun of it all.

The clock chimes jokes in a rhythm so sweet,
Tick-tock, tick-tock, and oh what a feat!
It tells of the times I was late with the pie,
'You needed a tutor,' the seconds all sigh.

A lonely chair hums with a zany refrain,
It knows every wobble, each creaky disdain.
Yet still, it insists on one dazzling spin,
As laughter erupts from the cupboards within.

In silence so rich, giggles start to unfold,
The very air shimmers with stories retold.
Voices come alive, full of whimsy and cheer,
In this quiet abode, no ghosts to fear!

The Unsaid Between the Stones

In corners dark, an echo stirs,
Old bricks gossip, like busy furs.
They chuckle 'bout the folks gone by,
With every creak, they wink and sigh.

A shoe from '89 left in haste,
Says it was fun—no time to waste!
A captain's hat, so worn and frayed,
Claims it was brave, yet so dismayed.

Cracks in the wall, a smile appears,
As tales unfold of laughter and cheers.
They share the blushes and puzzled looks,
With whispered secrets, like clever books.

So listen close, when silence reigns,
For in stillness, humor gains.
The stony hearts talk, oh what a treat,
In this silly game of memory's beat.

Traces of Time's Passage

Time rolls on, like a sigh on breeze,
Cracked paint laughs, it does as it please.
Old clocks can't keep the beat they once did,
And walls recall the kid who hid.

Echoes of shoes in a lively trot,
Dance with a rhythm, oh, what a plot!
A broom once struck a hole in the floor,
Now tells the tale of a silent roar.

With peeling posters and fading art,
Whispers of history play the part.
Ghosts of who wore the silly hat,
Still chuckle at the time that they sat.

So gather 'round, let laughter flow,
For each tiny crack has a story to show.
In the playful past, we find our way,
Through traces of joy, in sketches of gray.

Hidden Voices in Halls

In the hallways, voices giggle low,
With secrets tucked where no one will go.
Footsteps patter on dusty floors,
Each thump shares tales of mischievous roars.

A mop that thinks it's an artist's wand,
Paints silly stripes of the homespun bond.
While dust motes waltz in daring loops,
Chasing sunlight, like playful troops.

Whispers float from a forgotten shoe,
Claiming adventures they silently knew.
Giggles bounce off cracked porcelain,
While laughter loops, again and again.

So revel in the unnoticed cheer,
For every corridor holds a dear.
In shadows, the fun finds its place,
With hidden voices that wear a grin on their face.

The Pulse of Passageways

Listen keenly, the walls will speak,
With pulsing jokes that make you peek.
A hall with flair, a step to sway,
Hums a tune of the bright delay.

Tile to tile, a funny chat,
As each footprint sparks a spat.
A rogue sock from yesteryear's spree,
Claims it danced to a banjo's glee.

The air is thick with laughter's ring,
As tales interlace, what joy they bring!
Tomes of whispers, old and wizened,
Twist through passage, delight unhidden.

So frolic on through the playful lane,
For every step can spark a gain.
A dance of spirits, let them play,
In the pulse of these paths, they'll sway.

Dialogues in the Dust

In the corner, a spider spins,
Whispers of long-lost sins.
Dust bunnies form a lively crowd,
Arguing softly, oh so loud.

A chair creaks, an old friend sighs,
Sharing secrets, no goodbyes.
The window grins, a cheeky grin,
"What's the latest gossip? Do begin!"

A shelf shouts, "I'm more than just a place!"
Each book a tale, a silly race.
Lampshades giggle, their shades all askew,
Lighting the drama, a funny view.

Together they blend in a dusty dance,
Old tales retold, they take a chance.
With every creak and every groan,
The walls converse, a life of their own.

The Heartbeat of Old Structures

The walls hum softly, a funny tune,
Tickling the air like a playful balloon.
Floors laugh while squeaking in delight,
Making the night a whimsical sight.

Rug rats tumble, still full of cheer,
Whispering, "Don't let the adults hear!"
Creaky doors sway in a jolly jest,
Swinging wide with a twinkle, no rest.

Windows chuckle, sunbeams at play,
Casting shadows that dance and sway.
"Did you hear that?" the beams will tease,
"Let's spill some secrets, if you please!"

Brick by brick, they share a jest,
Each crack a wink, they're clearly blessed.
A structure's heart beats loud with fun,
Join the laughter, let's all run!

Silent Testaments

On the ceiling, a cobwebbed sage,
Critiques the antics of the modern age.
With every dust mote floating down,
The corners giggle, wearing a frown.

Potted plants eavesdrop, leaf by leaf,
Reporting back, causing some grief.
"My soil's better!" one pot will boast,
While another cracks jokes, laughing the most.

The fireplace grumbles, "I've seen it all,"
With tales of laughter echoing tall.
"Did you see that cat?" the mantle retorts,
"Now that's a story worth a few snorts!"

Within these walls, where spirits prance,
Laughter and whispers create a dance.
Silent but loud, they play their part,
Each echo a jest, each creak a heart.

Chronicles Embedded in Brick

Each brick a story, each crack a laugh,
Sketching out tales on a quirky path.
Walls discussing the weather and woes,
One laments rain, while another just glows.

A light fixture quips, shining so bright,
"Can you believe they turn me off at night?"
The pipes pipe up, bubbling with glee,
"Just wait, my friends, you'll see me!"

Beams stand tall, flexing with pride,
"Look at us all! We're built to abide!"
The floorboards joke, a wooden brigade,
"Let's dance till morning, don't be afraid!"

Laughter nesting in each colored hue,
Chalking up moments, old and new.
Echoes of humor in cracks, oh so thick,
In this merry home, it's magic, not trick.

Echo Chambers of Existence

In a room of whispers, secrets sway,
Chatter echoes, come what may.
The fridge hums tales of late-night snacks,
While the couch debates who lacks the hacks.

Laughter fills the air, wall to wall,
A sock's lost story makes them stall.
The clock ticks jokes, a silent band,
Tick-tock humor, isn't it grand?

Every knick-knack has a voice, I swear,
The lamp's glow gives life to fair.
"Who's stealing light?" the shadows chime,
As cushions confess to the best of crime.

At dusk, the walls trade their best retells,
With the rug's tales of its wear and smells.
Echoes dance in harmony, a waltz,
In this quirky home of funny faults.

The Secret Life of Wood

Once a tree, now planks so proud,
Wood whispers wonders, oh so loud.
The table's grumble, "I need some spice,"
While chairs just complain, "This isn't nice!"

Logs in logs, they're quite the crew,
Barking orders, who knew they'd do?
"Oh, to be a bird!" the beams do plead,
"Just one flight, then we can take heed!"

Nightly, they gossip, joined by some knots,
"Did you hear how the floor just forgot?"
A nail rolls by, claims it's the best,
Though squeaky planks are not impressed.

In the hands of the carver, stories arise,
Chiseled laughter, no need for disguise.
Wood and humor, an endless blend,
Life's funny tales, around each bend.

Reflections in Rusted Railings

The rusty railings blink and boast,
Of daring leaps and a foggy coast.
"Remember when the cat flew by?"
They recount while the pigeons sigh.

With a squeak and a creak, they share their fate,
Of birds who feast, and squirrels who wait.
"Do you see that kid? He's got some nerve!"
While the autumn leaves spin and curve.

The rails chuckle tales of missed delight,
Of lovers' whispers beneath the twilight.
Rusted memories form quite a tale,
As they giggle over last autumn's gale.

In the moonlight, they come alive,
With reflections that playfully connive.
Laughter echoes past tarnished sheen,
In these railings, humor is seen.

Hidden Histories Beneath the Surface

Beneath the floorboards, stories lie,
Of lost marbles and the dust bunny spy.
"Who needs a treasure map?" they jest,
"We've got more secrets than all the rest!"

The carpet rolls its eyes, so tired,
Of children's games that never expired.
"Stop jumping! I'm tired!" it giggles aloud,
While beneath it, the dust gathers proud.

Old pipes murmur secrets, warmth and cold,
In a plumbing debate, the tales unfold.
"Who took the sunshine?" they ask with glee,
As shadows dance, wanting to flee.

In a nook, the echoes collude by chance,
With the ghost of the cat, offering a dance.
Underneath the laughter, a world so grand,
In the hidden corners, we'll make our stand.

The Soul of the Space speaks

There's a cupboard that whispers quite loud,
It tells all the secrets of the crowd.
'Last Tuesday, they danced on the floor,'
'And I swear, I heard a small pig snore!'

The chandelier giggles, it sways and it hums,
It jangles with laughter, 'Oh look, here comes!'
Another guest slipping and tripping in style,
While I, the old sofa, just grin and compile.

The paintings on walls roll their eyes with delight,
'You think that's a dance? Oh dear, what a sight!'
Echoes of banter from days long ago,
Pillowed in corners, savor the show!

So come take a seat, join our merry brigade,
In this charming abode where memories parade.
With each laugh and story, the walls start to glow,
For it's all in the spirit—come, let's bestow!

Haunting Harmonies of History

The ghosts in the rafters are humming a tune,
They tap dance all night, under the craters of moon.
With a wink and a nudge, they jive and they swing,
Bringing back echoes of jokes from that fling.

A broom stands up straight, gets ready to glide,
It sweeps up mischief with supernatural pride.
And the clock on the wall chimes with mirthful chime,
Tick-tocking, it chuckles, feeling quite sublime.

The wallpaper peels, revealing a grin,
With old-fashioned quips tucked snugly within.
'Not that old carpet, it's a chair, not a rug!'
The quirks of this place give stretched smiles a tug!

So bring your best stories, the laughter won't cease,
Among spirits and shadows, you'll find your release.
In harmonies playful, let joy be your role,
For history's funny; it tickles the soul!

Custodians of Time

The old grandfather clock keeps a diary so neat,
Twelve tiny confessions hide under its feet.
'He tripped on his shoelace, what silliness there!'
'This chair once held court, it was quite the affair!'

Dust motes in the sunlight all swirl and laugh,
Reciting the tales of an awkward giraffe.
While a rug mumbles softly, 'I've heard it all,
Footsteps in sneakers, oh, how can they sprawl?'

In corners, a spider spins yarns of delight,
'Last week, they brewed a disaster tonight!'
With tales of spaghetti that flew through the air,
Custodians of time, they recall with great flair.

So stroll through this house, skip worries away,
Where memories mingle and frolic and play.
Embrace all the laughter that springs from the seams,
For these walls hold the fun of our wildest dreams!

Silent Witnesses of Laughter

In the nook of the room, the old chair does squeak,
It hums a bright tune of the funny and meek.
With each jolt and jerk, it revives a good jest,
The moments it saw are profoundly the best.

The lamp nods approvingly, casting soft light,
As visitors gather to share pure delight.
'Hey look at that fellow, so clumsy and spry!'
While hanging on hooks, coats chuckle and sigh.

A shadow darts past, oh was that a cat?
Or maybe the ghost that wore quite the hat?
With chuckles and giggles echoing wide,
These silent witnesses hold laughter inside.

So paint your own stories with laughter and cheer,
In the company of jesters who linger quite near.
For each whisper and rustle, each grin on the wall,
Turns this place into joy—come gather them all!

www.ingramcontent.com/pod-product-compliance
Lightning Source LLC
Chambersburg PA
CBHW070323120526
44590CB00017B/2792